IMAGES OF IRELAND

OLD BELLEEK TOWN

IMAGES OF IRELAND

OLD BELLEEK TOWN

JOE O'LOUGHLIN

NONSUCH

First published 2006

Nonsuch Limited
73 Lower Leeson Street
Dublin 2
www.nonsuch-publishing.com

National Library Cataloguing in Publication Data.
A catalogue record for this book is available from the National Library.

ISBN 1 84588 535 X

Typesetting and origination by Tempus Publishing Limited.
Printed in Great Britain.

Contents

Acknowledgements

Images of Ireland: Old Images of Belleek gives much valuable information on my native village, renowned worldwide for its Parian China. The village and the Erne waterways cannot be separated, so by word and picture it is my wish to pass on for posterity what this once proud river looked like many years ago. When in its elegant prime the Erne was considered to be one of the best fishing rivers in Europe. Famous for salmon, trout, eels and coarse fish it attracted anglers from far off lands.

The stories and the large number of photographs will for the more elderly reader recall forgotten memories of the days of yore. For the present and future generations it will give them an idea of how the district appeared to their forbearers. One does not need to be a native of the area to appreciate this work. This is my fifth publication and follows closely after the successful *Voices of the Donegal Corridor*, a book received with acclaim at home and abroad.

My academic qualifications are sparse to put it mildly. For the final period of my schooling I was placed in a section of the classroom reserved for those of us who in the highly valued opinion of the teacher had reached the outer limits of our learning ability. It is remarkable that a number of 'Graduates of the back seat Academy' became successful in their more mature years. One became a company director; another entered the political life and became the mayor of his adopted town. A young man who emigrated, furthered his education and became a lecturer in a regional college, his friend and comrade is now a successful business person. Of the young girls, they became, nurses, secretaries, bankers, teachers and gifted crafts persons in the china factory.

Like the scribe who would never let the truth come in the way of a good yarn, we should never let the lack of academic qualifications become a bar to success. Nevertheless we must remember to give credit to the teachers who in our formative years laid down the foundations for our chosen careers.

Finally I pay tribute to my faithful proof reader, Maire Carr, London, the writer of the preface, Michael McGrath of The Thatch Fishing Shop. To the editor, Noelle Moran for her professional help and expert advice so willingly given. To my growing number of readers who by asking the question, 'When is the next book coming out and what will it be about?' ensured that this work should be proceeded with. Joe is a Joint President of The Church Hill and Tully Castle Historical Society. A Committee member of The Clogher Historical Society and Vice- Chairman of The Association of Friends of the Fermanagh County Museum.

Preface

'Pleasant is the Erne and pleasant were its breezy days ......Could those days but come again, I would give the hopes of years for those bygone hours', Revd Henry Newland, 1850.

'The Erne, its fly fishing & its legends'

Everyone remembers and recalls the greater enjoyment of earlier, more youthful times in life. Before 1880 the Erne was a quiet and gentle waterway for sixty miles across the Northwest of Ireland – until it arrived in Belleek. There through the limestone gorge, violent cascading waterfalls and swirling pools emptied it down 160 feet into the Atlantic four miles away in Ballyshannon.

Between 1880 and 1890 leading - edge engineering, steam - driven boring tools, cordite, dynamite and many men removed 200,000 tons of rock from Belleek Falls and Rose Isle to create a magnificent cut stone barrier, across the river, with Sluice Gates. The fishermen were not happy – the natural salmon run was broken, the eels had to find a new route, the water was let through at the wrong times. Was the Erne for the fisherman, the Pottery grinding wheels, the farmers or for water transport?

Fifty years later 'they' took it all away, drained 6,500 acres up river and flooded 1,600 acres of cascading, swirling water by constructing two concrete hydro dams between Belleek and Ballyshannon in 1954. Thus the natural form of the Erne from time began, was disfigured twice in the last one hundred years. A Millennium before when the Vikings arrived, (the Lochlann's?... came with them!). They transported their boats overland from the sea, past the jumping salmon and thundering falls to Belleek. If they return in the future, new locks and lifts will bring them up past the dams. There might be more springing salmon, wriggling eels, and nautical natives on the waterways.

They are all very welcome to its idyllic vistas and wild nature.

Joe and I were reared on the banks of the Erne. In our youth we caught our first trout; we watched and listened to the water as time passed by.

'There is no river in the whole world like my first love, the Erne ...... Pleasant are its memories', Revd Henry Newland, 1850.

'Do I hear voices ......?' Michael P. McGrath

Introduction

For several century's and many generations since the written word came within the scope of the ordinary person many works on the River Erne and its beautiful lakes have been recorded in a variety of journals. The advent of photography has added a new dimension to an already interesting subject. Much of the work to date has consisted of a page here and a paragraph there by a variety of authors, it has to my mind been like the pieces of a jigsaw that needs assembling to enable one to get a clear view of the overall picture. Some years ago the late Mr Horace T Fleming gave me his treasured collection of photographs showing the River Erne as it was in its natural state before being changed forever by the engineers in the name of progress.

I remember the river as it was then; I consider myself privileged to have known it and to have listened to its voice. In the days of my youth I had listened to the older generation speak of the first Erne Drainage Scheme that had destroyed the great Falls of Belleek. I think that the time is now opportune to have all the stories and the photographs published in the one journal so that future generations can have some idea of the beauties of this part of their homeland. It is said that one picture is equal to one thousand words. Therefore I will let this collection of pictures of the Old River Erne speak for themselves.

The village of Belleek is as old as the average Irish assembly of dwellings, founded by the Caldwell landlord family at the place of the 'Flagstone Ford' from which it derives its name. This ford was the first crossing point on the Erne west of Enniskillen and for centuries was the gateway between Ulster and Connaught. It was of course of strategic importance when the warring clans of the provinces tried to get control of each others territory. Over the years and especially during the last half of the century, the appearance of the village has been altered in the name of progress. Where once the local farms almost bordered the main street, development of housing has expanded the village into what was once valuable agricultural land. Again I am letting the photographs tell their own story in their own way so the present generation can see for themselves what the landscape looked like in the olden days.

The world famous Belleek Parian China factory has ensured that the village is known the world over. The word 'Belleek' is listed in the Webster Dictionary.

Before the invention of the wheel and the development of overland transport, the waterways of Ireland were the highways of the island. The earliest vessels were dugout canoes used by the natives to move from one part of their territory to another including the fertile islands of Lough Erne. In the 1950s, during a particularly dry spell of weather, there was a considerable drop in the level of the lake with the result that several canoes were discovered and recovered from their resting place of centuries. The Irish had a rather clever way of safeguarding their vessels when they came ashore to travel inland, they filled the canoe with stones to sink it beneath the surface. On their return the stones were removed and the vessel was seaworthy again. No pay and display for parking then!

The first sail powered craft to be seen on the Erne were most likely the Viking longboats. The Vikings came ashore at Ballyshannon only to find that the river could not accommodate their ships. Scouts were sent inland to explore the land and it did not take long to discover that the river became a large lake near where the village of Belleek now is. They sailed in fleets of several longboats on their adventures; each boat was up to twenty metres in length with a beam of five metres. Normally they carried a crew of thirty sailors who were expert oarsmen to propel the boat in calm weather. The prow and stern were of the same design so it was not necessary to turn the boat to change direction. The oarsmen just faced the opposite way in their seats or else the sail was adjusted to suit the direction of travel. The ocean going boats had a long deep keel; others were designed with a flat bottom for shallow waters and for moving them over frozen rivers and lakes.

The boats were taken ashore at Ballyshannon; tree trunks were cut to act as rollers to move them over land to Belleek. There it was a simple matter to re-launch them when they sailed up the lake to plunder the Fermanagh monasteries and subdue the native Irish. They first came here in 837 and off and on remained for 200 years. In 924 one raiding party spent the winter months at Caol Uisce or narrow waters as the river was called. The next foreigners to come to Fermanagh were the Normans, for them the Ford was very important from a military point of view. Gilbert De Costella built the first fort on the Cloghore cliff top in 1211. It was a wooden structure and was destroyed by fire during an attack in 1212. The site lay idle until 1252 when the Normans built a replacement fort. Godfrey O'Donnell destroyed this structure within a short time and expelled the Normans from the area for the last time.

Mention is made of Belleek again in 1689 when Patrick Sarsfield was in the area with a view to taking Ballyshannon. Reinforcements were on their way from Enniskillen to support Captain Henry Folliott who was in command of the Ballyshannon garrison. The wooden bridge at Belleek was described as a great pass between the provinces of Ulster and Connaught. So Sir John Caldwell had the bridge destroyed and with his men he now controlled all the fords on the river. Lieutenant Colonel Thomas Loyd was in command of the troupes marching from Enniskillen to Ballyshannon along the south bank of the river. When Loyd came near Belleek he was faced with a large tract of bog land that his cavalry and infantry found it impossible to cross. Sarsfield controlled the firm land. A local man came to the rescue of Loyd, he knew of the existence of a causeway over the swamp. He guided the troups safely across and so Loyd got to Ballyshannon in time to secure the town.

One of the most outstanding boats to ply on the lakes was the 'Devenish'. Described as the biggest and best of the Lough Erne boats she was launched on Friday, 26 July 1862 by the Lough Erne Steamboat Company. Built in sections by Henderson Colbourne of Renfrew, Scotland, at a cost of £3,700 pounds. The sections were brought to the Market Yard, Enniskillen, where the Scottish riveters assembled them. That was quite an exciting time for the people of Enniskillen as they watched the red hot rivets fitting together the steel plates that formed the hull. The Devenish was 131 feet long with a beam of 16 feet; powerful twin engines drove her two big paddle wheels. She could carry almost 1,000 passengers and cargo, for a large vessel she had a shallow draft of two feet, two inches. She could do the trip from Enniskillen to Belleek in two and a half hours including stops on the way.

She plied successfully on the Erne for six years, but the coming of the railways heralded the end of shipping on the lake. The Devenish was sold in 1869 to John Brown & Company of Bangor, County Down. There are two stories of how she was moved to Bangor, one being that she was partially dismantled and transported by rail to Bangor. This does not seem practical; as many of the low bridges along the railway would not have had the necessary clearance for a high load. The account given by Mervyn Dane in history in the Impartial Reporter of 24 September 1970 is more sensible:

'She was probably stripped of her engines and other equipment to reduce weight and hauled overland from the Erne at Belleek. Then began the tortuous overland journey to the sea at Ballyshannon on flat bogeys drawn by horses or oxen. The roads were not suitable for such a heavy load and there were frequent holdups as wheels bogged down. The slow journey proceeded and the *Devenish* was launched into the sea again at Ballyshannon. Then taken to Belfast for a refit, she was given the new name of '*The Lady of the Lake*' and plied daily between Belfast and Hollywood, County Down'.

In 1873 the nine year old paddle steamer from Lough Erne was sold again, hoisted aboard a cargo ship and brought to the west coast of Africa where there was a demand for paddle steamers with a shallow draft to work on the rivers along the coast.

THE VOICE OF THE RIVER ERNE

It is a long way back that I am gazing
The Erne has changed since then
Oh! Memory – that midway world
Between Earth and Paradise
Where things decayed and loved ones lost
Now in dreary shadows rise
Before the engineers straightened out
The Winding Banks of Erne

one

The Erne Rivers and Lakes

'We pay tribute here to that once beautiful and famous river whose appearance has been destroyed forever in the false name of progress. Its lost landscape can never be replaced. When some future generation has invented a much simpler method than ours of getting power, light and heat, let not the dry, stained bed of the Erne bear witness to the insanity and ruthless vandalism of our time'. Only the prose of that era, as used by William Allingham the famous Ballyshannon poet, can fully describe the beauty of the river and its scenic surroundings. The four-mile stretch of river from Belleek to the estuary was unsurpassed in the amazing variety of its beauty. Its swift flowing waters with its gurgling noise and cascading silver spray dancing in the sunlight of a summer's day, a scene of beauty unequalled in its loveliness. The thunder of the water over the falls and through the rapids near Belleek had been called the '*Voice of the Erne*'.

The old Erne as it made its way gently and silently from Lough Gowna in Cavan, through Fermanagh, between the ancient Kingdoms of Mulleek and Toura only found its *Voice* when it reached the falls at Belleek. For those who had the gift to listen, the *Voice* could be heard from there to the sea. It is easy to imagine the thoughts of a fisherman, as listening to the *Voice*; he cast his line and flies into the pools that lay below the rapids and between the winding banks of the Erne. He knew that hidden from his view to the east lay the great broad lake with its many wooded islands under the watchful eye of the mountain named the Barr of Wealt. From Belleek, on its westward way it dropped rapidly past thick copses where large trees mingled on the waterside. A small well-wooded park in that region called Camlin seemed to be the very type of rich sylvan beauty that formed pictures in the imagination of the wonderful landscape that lay beyond the riverbanks.

The river finally made its way to the broad Atlantic Ocean where its next neighbours, away in the sunset, are the lands of America and Canada. In that new world many emigrants from the Erne valley found a new life, they departed from the Mall Quay at Ballyshannon in ill equipped vessels on that hazardous journey into the unknown. Sad were the scenes of parting on the quay, emigration was small in the early part of the eighteenth century compared to what it became in later years. The fare was but a few pounds, often sent from the New World by those who were already settled there. Though the partings were sad, no one was ever heard to complain of the dangers that lay ahead. One thing that lingered forever in the memory of those on board the ships was the sound of the *Voice* of the River Erne. To the south, the river was guarded by the high mountains of Sligo and Leitrim with their hidden glens, reputedly the home of Allingham's fairies. To the north the peaks and hills of Donegal with its rugged farmlands kept watch over the great river.

The colour of these hills changed all the time in the light of the sun. The sky arches over it all, giving at night, room to multitudes of stars, while by day; a long procession of clouds is blown inland from the sea. Also to the south lay the Moy Plain, the scene of many an ancient fight or foray. Great as are all these beauties of nature, nothing impressed so much as the sound – *The Voice* – that ceased not by day or by night. The hum could be heard of the water going over the falls, rolling continually over the rocky ledges into deep pools beneath. In some modes the river sounded like ever-flowing time itself made audible.

The pools beneath the bridge of Belleek were the chief scenes of fishing so important to the village. Summer idlers had an untiring pleasure lounging on the arches of the bridge, or on the green banks. To watch the fishermen swiftly casting out and slowly but expertly playing their catch to the sound of the ratchet of a big brass reel and the rod itself bent the shape of a rainbow as the line took the strain, this was the Erne as I remember it, as God created it, sadly now replaced by dead water – water that has no sound and no *Voice*. But then it is a long way back that I am gazing and the river has changed since then, before the engineers forever silenced the *Voice* of the River Erne.

two

Lower Lough Erne

Any writing on the River Erne would not be complete without a description of the mother lake. Again I return to the period of 125 years ago and use the style of the period as used by Revd H N Lowe, an English author and fisherman...

A fine river, and two large magnificent lakes, the former chiefly, and the later almost wholly in County Fermanagh. The river issues from Lough Ganny or Gawna, on the mutual border of the Counties of Longford and Cavan; and runs north-west through the latter county, beautifying much of it with locustrine expansions and sylvan and meadowy meanderings, and receiving in its progress the tribute of the Cootehill and Woodford rivers, and of various minor streams.

The Erne only drops two feet from the east of Fermanagh until it reaches the Belleek Falls. The drop from the fall to the estuary at Ballyshannon is a remarkable 150 feet. From the foot of the Lower Lake Erne to Donegal Bay, it has a westerly run of two and a half miles in County Fermanagh, and five and a half miles across the extremity of the southern wing of County Donegal; and it sweeps athwart a considerable amount of fine scenery and makes a great rapid at Belleek, a splendid cataract at Ballyshannon, and two or three intermediate accelerations of current.

Upper Lough Erne, the middle or connecting reach of the River Erne, and Lower Lough Erne unitedly extend north-westward, from end to end of County Fermanagh, and very nearly along its middle, so as to cleave it into two almost equal longitudal sections by a vast and very varied aqueous basin. Swells, undlaions, diversified slopes, and isolated limestone hills, form the greatest part of both the margin and the sky-line of the grand valley; but, on the other hand, low marshy, and meadowy flats, broadly fringe a considerable portion of both the upper and connecting reach of the river, and the Poola Fooka range of table-land, rising to an altitude of above 1,000 feet, flanks a very large proportion of the Lower Lough.

'Lough Erne, round its whole circumference', says Mr Ingles. 'Does not offer one tame and uninteresting view; everywhere there is beauty, and beauty of a very high order. In some places the banks are thickly wooded to the water's edge. In other places, the fairest and smoothest slopes rise from the margin, shaping themselves into knolls and green velvety lawns; here and there finely wooded promontories extend far into the lake, forming calm, sequestered inlets and bays; and sometimes a bold foreground, not perhaps of mountains, but of lofty hills, juts forth, and contrasts finely with the richness and cultivation on either side.

And what shall I say of the numerous islands, far more numerous than those on Windermere, and as beautiful as the most beautiful of them; some of them densely covered with wood, some green and swelling, and some large enough to exhibit the richest union of wood and lawn;

some laid out as pleasure ground, with pleasure houses for those to whom they pertain; and some containing the picturesque ruins of ancient and beautiful edifices. Nor must I forget the magnificent mansions that adorn the banks of Lough Erne, and which add greatly to the general effect of the landscape. I shall not easily forget, nor would I ever wish to forget, the delightful hours I one day spent on the shore of this more than Windermere of Ireland.

It was a day of uncommon beauty; the islands seemed to be floating on a crystal sea; the wooded promontories threw their broad shadows half across the still bays; the fair slopes and lawny knolls stood greenly out from amongst the dark sylvan scenery that intervened; here and there a little boat rested on the bosom of some quiet cove; and in some of the shallow bays, or below the slopes of some of the green islands, cattle stood single or in groups in the water. I confidently assert that Lower Lough Erne, take it all in all, is the most beautiful lake in the Three Kingdoms, but for the majestic Alpine outline that bounds the horizon on the upper part of Lake Leman, Lake Leman itself could not contend in beauty with this little-visited lake in the County of Fermanagh'.

(Lake Leman is a beautiful lake at the foot of the Swiss Alps. Lowe gives the name 'Poola Fooka' meaning the Hole of the Demons, to the Barr of Wealt mountain range that overlooks Lower Lough Erne. Having in June 2005 made a flight in a micro light plane over Lough Erne, I must say that his description of the lake, its islands and surrounding landscape is exactly as I viewed it from above.)

three

Belleek – The Village

Following the Battle of Ballinamuck and the victory of the English forces led by General Lake, a decision was made to build a permanent fort and a new bridge at Belleek. These were to replace the wooden structures that had been destroyed in earlier conflicts. In charge of the construction was Sir William Augustus Smith B T this London born officer had served as a Captain in the Essex Fencibles and for thirty-five years had been an engineer in the Lough Swilly District during which period the Towers and Batteries on Lough Swilly and Lough Foyle were constructed.

There is a letter from him dated 19 May 1827 in the Public Records Office in London concerning a disputed boundary to the Ordinance land at Belleek. From the letter it is clear that Sir William supervised the construction of Belleek Fort and he mentions in the letter that he had received an order to lay out the covered embrasures so as in the darkest night to command all the fords and that he had several picturesque drawings made by himself after the work was complete. Twenty nine years after the construction of the fort he was able to provide personal testimony to settle the dispute while still serving at the age of seventy seven.

There was a sequel with local connections to the Battle of Ballinamuck, County Longford on the 8 September 1798, during which the combined forces of the United Irishmen and the French were defeated. Three young men escaped from the battlefield and made their way northwards. They were Peter Duffy from Glenalunn; which is to the south of the River Erne, Patrick McGoldrich from Gadalough; which is north of the river and Hugh Ward who was from the west of Ireland. After over a year traveling overland the three fugitives reached the Duffy home in November 1799, where they rested for some time. Duffy remained at home while Ward and McGoldrich made their way to the river; there they found a boat that they used to cross to the north shore. They rested in a cabin but they were warned that a group of Yeomen led by Sir John Caldwell was searching for them.

McGoldrich escaped over the rugged moorland, Ward decided to make for the river. Being a strong swimmer he chose to take to the water at Downey's Point on the Lowery shore to swim across to Roscor Island. Sadly he was shot by a local Yeoman as he swam to the island. Some time later his body was recovered by local people who buried him on a small island near the Caldwell estate. To this day the island is known as Dead Man's or Lonesome Island and it as marked as such on the maps of the lake.

In 1880 after the construction of the railway and the founding of Belleek Pottery, H N Lowe describes the village as a most prosperous and thriving little town in the parish of the same name, and in the barony of Lurg. The Erne River, after escaping from Lough Erne, rolls swiftly two and a half miles to Belleek, and passing the prosperous and extensive porcelain works of Messrs

D McBirney & Co., and there giving the aid of its powerful force in working their ponderous machinery, it forms a noble cataract, equivalent in average mechanical power to 15,000 horses. In summer the town is much frequented by tourists and anglers, as there is excellent sport on the river; and the site of the town most picturesque and healthy, partly, it is presumed, in consequence to Bundoran.

There are two eel weirs close to the town, one about two miles upstream in Druminillar, the other about one mile downstream. Several ton weight of these fish have often been caught in less than one hour at night. Cliff, the delightful detached residence of the Conolly family, is close to the town. Newman states in his writing that an average of 60 tons of eels could be taken from the Erne in a year. To give an idea of the value of eel fishing the Ordinance Survey carried out in 1830 records that Druminillar eel weir was set to Mr Johnston for £115-0-0 and Conolly's weir at Belleek, Cora Dermot, was set for £122-0-0 per annum. The Erne at Belleek was very deep above and below the falls, it narrows from 150 yards above the falls to 50 yards below. There were three islands on the river at the falls, White Isle, Rose Isle and Belleek Isle. An eel weir was also situated there. The catch of salmon was equally great. In 1825, 76 tons of salmon were taken from the Erne. Is it any wonder then that Sir Humprey Davy said, 'I should place the Erne as now the first river for salmon fishing from the banks with a rod, in the British Dominion'.

The Rogan family of Belleek and Ballyshannon were renowned the world over for their skills in tying flies. The expert angler would carry his supply of flies on his headgear, usually a tweed hat. Other fishermen would study the hat in order to find out which was the best fly to use at a particular time. One rather cute angler would place on his hat a collection of the most useless flies possible to lead his rivals astray.

In 1880 the once famous Belleek water falls were blasted out of existence by that latest of inventions — dynamite. The purpose of the exercise was to relieve flooding in east Fermanagh by dredging the river from Roscor to Belleek. A set of sluice gates were erected, they were a wonderful piece of mechanism, designed by Mr F Stoney, C E, for the Lough Erne Drainage and Navigation Board for the purpose of regulating the waters of the Upper and Lower lakes. The River Erne, from the mouth of the Lower Lake to Belleek, a distance of three miles, had its bed deepened and all the fords taken away, as was the Druminillar eel weir. The improvement of Lough Erne had long been an object contemplated by the Government and also by the landed proprietors and merchants of the neighbourhood. As steamers had by now started to operate on the lake, this meant that they could operate all the year round between Belleek and Enniskillen. They could do this because the level of the lake could be controlled in all seasons. With the building of the Ulster Canal, direct water communication was possible from Belleek to Belfast.

There is an amusing story about a family that lived on Lowery shore where the lake becomes a river. In the O'Neill family there were five pretty sisters who were traditional Irish dancers. Out from the shore there was a large shelf of rock that was only a few inches beneath the surface. When steamers were passing by, the girls would go onto the flat rock and give an exhibition of Irish folk dancing much to the puzzlement of the passengers on the vessels who were not aware that the water was very shallow...

Mr J G V Porter of Bellisle, Lisbellaw, put on a steamer for tourists on Lough Erne, leaving Enniskillen daily at 10 am, arriving at Belleek at 12.45 pm, and returning at 3.45 pm, reaching Enniskillen in time for trains to Sligo, Omagh and Derry. The Quay for the steamers was on the south shore of the river in the town land of Corry. The Harbour Master, Kernaghan's house was eventually bought in 1925 by Thomas O'Loughlin and it was there that the author was born. Apart from transport for travelers and fishermen, the Erne was a trade highway before the construction of roads. In the early 1800s Ballyshannon was a thriving port, cargo for Fermanagh such as iron, lead, slates, timber, coal and the Portland stone used to build several of the castles came there on the ships. It was transported to Belleek by wagon and loaded unto steamers at Kernaghan's Quay to be brought to Enniskillen and other places. Transport cots also conveyed goods from Belleek to Enniskillen. They were wooden structures capable of carrying about 18 tons, generally they carried mast and sail, and were fitted with sets of oars, a paddle was fixed to the stern to steer the vessel with. Some were 55 feet long, 10 feet wide and over 5 feet deep. They were used to carry turf from Belleek and sand from Castle Caldwell, Rossharbour and Lusty More to Enniskillen. Special cots were used to bring cattle out to the fertile islands on the lake.

four

Fishing on the Erne

The Erne Fishery Company was formed in the late 1800s and it was managed by Mr R L Moore of Derry, who had bought Cliff House, the Donegal residence of Thomas Conolly, MP, it was situated about one mile down stream from Belleek. The Druminillar eel weir gives the name to the town land of Corrakeel on the south shore of the river; Corrakeel means the place of the weir. About midway between Belleek and Cliff House there was an eel weir known as Corra Dermott, below Cliff House were three eel weirs known as Corra Bawn, Corra Donnel and Corra Monagh. Between the Kathleen Falls and Ballyshannon bridge was situated the final eel weir, Corra Shane. The last five were lost when the dams were built in the late 1940s.

Eels spend four to eight years of their lives in lakes, ponds, ditches, streams and rivers, the mature eels then make their way to the sea as spawning time approaches. They usually travel on dark stormy autumn nights and it is at this time that they are caught in nets set in the weirs. On reaching the ocean they commence their journey to the Sargasso Sea in the mid-Atlantic, where the eggs are laid, the adult eel then dies. The elvers, young eels, swim back to the fresh water rivers where their parents came from, traveling up to 4,000 miles. A mature eel can grow up to 3 feet long.

Belleek has always been famous for its eels, local women are said to be the best in the world in the art of eel cooking. The poor always looked to fish for their food, they never fished for sport. The salted eel was the staple food for the people who lived near the Erne. The catching of eels and other fish may explain why the numbers who died during the Great Famine were not as great here as in other areas. Salmon never travel at night, when they reach the ocean they swim to their breeding ground in the north Atlantic, they return yearly to their original rivers and streams. Salmon travel in 'schools', the leader of the school is a mature fish known as 'The School Master'.

The Abbott of the Cistercian Abbey Assaroe at Ballyshannon had for centuries held the fishing rights for salmon, trout and eels from the estuary to the Lower Lake. Following the Plantation of Ulster the English planter families took control of the fishing rights. In the early 1900s the claims of the landlords were contested in the courts. In 1933 the commercial fishermen of Ballyshannon and district won the right under license to net salmon on the estuary.

On 19 March 1903, Thomas McGahan and Edward McGrady of South Carolina, U.S.A. who had acquired the Caldwell estate sold their interest in it to the Revd Edward Parr of Surrey, England. Details of the fishing rights were included in the legal agreement:

'The following fisheries and rights of fishing, so far as they affect the lands herein before granted, that is to say firstly the Salmon Fishery or Fishery for Salmon by nets, loops, weirs or otherwise howsoever from

the Bar of Ballyshannon in the County of Donegal in and through the whole extent of the River Erne and the waters thereof and the river commonly called the Abbey River near by Ballyshannon aforesaid and the waters thereof and all other rivers and water courses having communication with the said Rivers Erne and Abbey where salmon are known to breed and cast spawn and all and singular the Salmon Fishery and liberty and right of taking salmon formerly belonging to Thomas Conolly in and upon the said Rivers Erne and Abbey and in and upon all rivulets, creeks and waters near or belonging thereto in the counties of Donegal, Fermanagh and Cavan or any or either of them with liberty of making and erecting new weirs in all convenient parts of the said rivers for taking salmon and also the eel fishing or fishery for eels at or near the town of Ballyshannon and all and singular the royalties and liberty and right of taking eels formerly belonging to the said Thomas Conolly or near the town of Ballyshannon aforesaid with all and singular the right members privileges and appurtenances to the said salmon and eel fisheries belonging or appertaining with liberty of erecting and making new weirs in all convenient parts of the said eel fishery and secondly the fishery and fisheries and liberty and right of fishing for and taking herrings of all other kinds of fish whatsoever by nets, lops, weirs or otherwise howsoever formerly belonging to the said Thomas Conolly in or within the entire creek, bay, harbour, channel and waters of Ballyshannon in the county of Donegal from the High Sea in and through the whole of the River Erne and the waters thereof and the river commonly called the Abbey River near Ballyshannon aforesaid and the waters thereof and all other rivers and waters having communication with the said Rivers Erne and Abbey and all the several★ fisheries formerly belonging to the said Thomas Conolly in the said waters and every part thereof together with all water ways, water courses, rights, members privileges and appurtenances to the said fisheries and premises belonging or in anywise appertaining situate in the Counties of Donegal , Fermanagh and Cavan. Included is the Salmon Fishery or fishing for salmon by loops or otherwise in or near the Fall of Belleek in the Counties of Donegal and Fermanagh or either of them and all and singular the royalties salmon fishery and liberty and right of taking salmon of Major John Colpoys Bloomfield and William Maffett as receiver over the estates and of the said Thomas Conolly as their Grantee in and upon the River Erne and in and upon all rivulets and creeks or waters near or belonging thereto in the counties of Donegal, Fermanagh and Cavan'.

★'Several' is a legal term for fisheries not common to two or more landlords.
★Free fishing is for all persons.

The legal document contains a considerable amount of further details much of which is a repeat of the above. What is quoted gives a good general idea of the lucrative salmon and eel fishing rights legally held by the landlords of the period.

At some period in the 1800s the Erne Fishery Company was formed and it acquired the fishery rights for the Erne. The company would on demand and without charge issue a permit to 'Angle for Trout'. An illustration shows a copy of a permit issued by the Bailiff on behalf of the Erne Fishery Company to Thomas Beacon of Belleek on 29 May 1897 to the 19 day of August 1897. A later permit excluded the section of the river from 'The Mullans' to the Eel Weir below Belleek, known as Johnston's. No bait but fly of a limited size allowed. Conditions on the back of the permit stated; 'No Angling on Sunday nor at any time at the Flag, in the Pool, Trout Hole, Boxes, Stream or Island. No salmon, salmon fry, jenkins, or eel fry to be taken or interfered with. No salmon throw to be fished. No injury to be done to growing crops or fences on the banks of the river.' Local history tells that the late Edward Thornhill; a local angler took a case to the courts claiming the right for the people to fish for trout on the Erne. It is said that he had the backing of local clergy and that the case finally went to the House of Lords where it was found in his favour. Research is still ongoing on the matter. The fact is that the right to free fishing for trout was granted at some stage, as the permit above testifies.

five

An Erne Fishery Case

The following case was reported in a local paper on 13 September 1900:

An important fishery prosecution was heard at Belleek Petty Sessions, on Tuesday, 11 September 1900, before Mr Smith, R M, Chairman, and six County Fermanagh magistrates. The case was brought by summons under the name of Michael McCormick, water-keeper, against James Quinn, for fishing on Lough Erne without the permission of the lessee of the alleged several fisheries. Mr R Ross Todd, solicitor, appeared to prosecute, and Mr M Maguire defended Quinn. The fishing was not denied by the defendant. The summons was brought under 11th and 12th Vic. Chap. 92, sec. 41, 14 and Vic. Chap. 98. Mr Ross Todd relied on a similar case on the opposite side of the river decided by Judge Craig, at Enniskillen, on appeal from the same petty sessions. Mr Todd produced a copy of inquisition under Charles 1, in 1649 and the patent two years later to the predecessor of the Marquis of Ely. Mr Maguire relied on the difference between a free fishery and a several fishery. The majority of the Bench dismissed the case on the merits and Mr Todd at once appealed.

The Revd Henry Newland in his writings of 1850 lists the Salmon Throws as mentioned above, he also provided a map of the Erne showing the throws. They are as follows from Belleek downstream:

1 - The Belleek Pool.
2 - The Rose Isle Throw.
3 - The Monks Ford.
4 - The Point of the Mullans.
5 - The Bank of Ireland.
6 - The Black Rock.
7 - The Sally Bush.
8 - The Tail of the Island.
9 - The Fox's Throw.
10 - The Mois Ruah.
11 - The Earls Throw.
12 - The Captains Throw.
13 - The Cursed Throw.
14 - Johnston's Throw.
15 - The Grass Guard.
16 - The Sod Ditch.

17 – The Eel Weir.
18 – Cos na Wonna.
19 – The Readers Throw.
20 – Kathleen's Falls.
21 – The Great Pool of Ballyshannon.

It is said that the fairies of the Erne Valley are of a milder and better nature than most other fairies. They exhibit no envious feelings whatever, but on Fridays they return to their subterraneous hills and pass the day in weeping and bemoaning their fate. The Irish Fairies are the Fallen Angels who were judged not good enough to remain in Heaven but not bad enough to be condemned to Hell. Pat Gallagher of Belleek was an expert fiddle player; he was also a keen fisherman. Often while waiting for the May Fly to take he would pass the time playing the fiddle as he sat on the riverbank. One dusky evening he was playing a haunting melody when a fairy appeared beside him. The Little Man was so enchanted by the music that to show his appreciation he gave Pat a magic fishing fly with the warning that he was never to tell anyone about it. Naturally Pat had many fine catches with the fly, then one day after indulging in drinking some poteen he told a friend about the fly and thereafter he lost the fly and the power to catch great fish. Poteen is a home brewed spirit known as, 'The Mountain Dew'.

six

A Lough Erne Ballad

The story of the Erne would not be complete if it did nor include at least one Ballad from the district. Some years ago my brother Pat got a cassette of Hilly Billy songs from America, with it was the story of how the author discovered the Ballad of *'The Blooming Bright Star of Belle Isle'*. Belle Isle is a well known island on Upper Lough Erne.

I was rummaging through an old *'Sing Out!'* (1957 – Summer), an American magazine, containing music and lyrics of folk songs, when I came across this lovely song. *'Sing Out!'* gave no credit to its source, however, which proved to be Fowke and Johnston's Folk Songs of Canada. It was collected by Kenneth Peacock in 1952 and was later printed in his 1965 book, *'Songs of the Newfoundland Outports'*. The last two verses that I sing were not in the *'Sing Out!'* version, but they were sent to me by Joe Hicherson, who found them in Greenleaf's *'Ballads and Songs of Newfoundland'*. The theme of the song suggests a kinship to the many 'broken token' songs, where a lover returns in disguise to test the faithfulness of his sweetheart. I've always thought that a gutsy thing to do, as well as being a dirty trick. I'm sure one can find other, more enjoyable ways to test things. Or perhaps it served as protection for the man who, if he saw his old love no longer cared, could walk away without having to face her.

The Blooming Bright Star of Belle Isle

One evening for pleasure I rambled
To view the fair fields all alone,
Down by the banks of Loch Erne
Where beauty and pleasure were known.

I spied a fair maid at her labour
Which caused me to stay for a while.
I thought her the Goddess of beauty,
The blooming bright star of Belle Isle.

I humbled myself to her beauty.
'Fair maid, where do you belong?
Are you from the heavens descended?
Abiding in Cupid's fair throng?'

'Young man, I will tell you a secret.
'Tis true I'm a maid that is poor,
And to part from my vows and my promise
Is more than my heart can endure'.

'Therefore, I'll remain at my labour
And go through all hardship and toil,
And wait for the lad who has left me
All alone on the banks of Belle Isle.'

'Fair maiden, I wish not to banter.
'Tis true I came here in disguise.
I came to fulfill my last promise
And hoped to give you a surprise'.

'I own you're the maid I love dearly;
You've been in my heart all the while.
For me there is no other damsel
Than the blooming bright star of Belle Isle.'

Now then this young couple gets married
In wedlock they both join in hand.
May the great God of Heaven protect them,
And give them long life on the land.

May the great God of Heaven protect them,
Loyalty be theirs all the while,
And honey will sweeten the comforts
For the blooming bright star of Belle Isle.

It is remarkable that this song which was obviously penned in Fermanagh should find its way to Newfoundland, from there to the southern states of America and then back again to Lough Erne's green shores well over a hundred years later.

seven

Mr Horace T Fleming

Mr Fleming was an eminent surgeon who for many years was attached to the Fermanagh County Hospital in Enniskillen. He was there during the turbulent years of the Second World War, when he treated many airmen who were injured in aircraft crashes. To get some relaxation from his taxing profession in the hospital Mr Fleming would spend two weeks fishing on the River Erne usually in the month of May when the May fly was in season. He did not specialize in any particular surgical department; he was skilled in all types of surgery.

Some people will wonder that he held the title 'Mister', there is a historical background to this. It the early years of medical care the normal medical doctor cared for the usual ills of his patients. Any person requiring surgery such as having an arm or a leg removed went to the local barber who performed the task, without any form of anesthetic other than a large shot of alcohol. The pole outside the barber shop was and still is a pole painted in stripes of red and white. This indicated the blood and bandages associated with his medical side line.

Naturally the barber was considerably lower down the social scale than a Medical Doctor; therefore he was called 'Mister'. Gradually the system changed and with progress medical doctors trained and became proficient in surgery and replaced the barber. Within a few years they climbed above the doctor on the social ladder, but if they did, they retained the title 'Mister' as a sign of their superior standing in the medical profession.

Cork born Horace Fleming would always stay in Mackey's Guest House, on Cliff Road, during his fishing vacation. When the trout were not taking, he would get his camera and take photographs of his beloved River Erne. He lived in retirement until he was well over ninety years of age. Shortly before he died and when he was still in excellent health he expressed a wish to have his photograph collection donated to the Belleek community. I was delegated to meet him in has home and carry out this wish.

Over several visits during which we talked about our common interests in Belleek and the river, he gave me his collection and instructions on how the pictures should be displayed in the village for the pleasure of the local residents. With the help of the Irvinestown historian, Breege McCusker, I organized a photographic exhibition in the Carlton Hotel. We had over 400 photos on exhibit including many from private collections. On the night a full framed set of the Fleming collection of photographs were presented to a selection of premises used by the public.

The original photographs were placed in the care of The Fermanagh County Museum in Castle Barracks, Enniskillen. The Fleming Collection inspired me to produce this book to record in writing and picture a history of the Erne and its three rivers. The first after rising on the Longford/ Cavan border flows to Fermanagh and there forms Upper Lough Erne. It becomes a river once again to flow through the Island Town of Enniskillen and there close to Devenish Island broadens itself to form Lower Lough Erne. At the west end of Fermanagh it becomes a river for the final time between the Lowery Bane and Roscor shores. This last stage of the river flows for almost eight miles to enter the Atlantic Ocean at Ballyshannon.

There is a vast amount of history about Belleek and I have many photographs to go along with it. Most of the pictures have never been published before and many of the stories have not appeared together in one book. I have resisted the temptation to include a detailed history of Belleek in this journal; rather I have chosen to concentrate on the River Erne, the lake and the valley for they deserve a work of their own.

Belleek Bridge and the Fort as it was in 1800. Painting – Jane O'Loughlin.

The winding River Erne from Belleek to the Lower Lake overlooked by the Barr of Wealt or Poola Fooka.

Belleek Pottery and the Old Bridge. Painting – Joseph McLoughlin.

The Sluice Gates – designed by Mr Storey, C E who also designed the Manchester Shipping Canal. Picture taken after the 1880 drainage.

Above: The Rapids, the Old Bridge and Belleek Village, 1949.

Right: Cliff generation station. It changed for ever the River Erne.

A sunset over the Erne Estuary from the Mall Quay from where sailing ships carried emigrants to the new world.

Edward and Benny Campbell stand a long way out on the frozen surface of the lake at Drumbad shore, 1947.

Opposite: Bernard Campbell, Edward Campbell and Patrick Timoney stand on the frozen surface of Lough Erne during the severe frost of 1947.

Roscor Bridge – built 1926. Where the lake becomes a river for the last time.

P J Slevin boating on the Erne at Roscor Bridge.

Above: The largest vessel to come to Belleek since the days of the steamers, in the nineteenth century. This converted barge sailed from Belgium, to Limerick, up the River Shannon, the Ballyconnell Canal, the full length of the Erne Waterway to Belleek Marina, 1996.

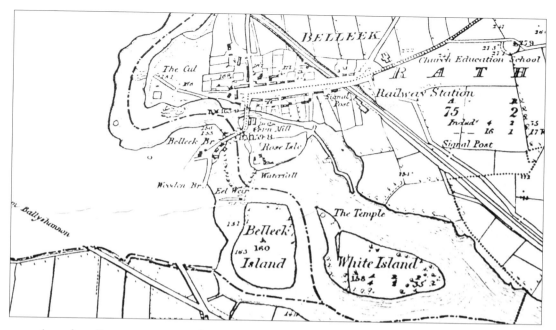

An early ordinance survey map of Belleek, before the 1880 drainage scheme. See the three islands – White Island, Belleek Island and Rose Isle. Also the famous Waterfall and an eel weir.

The Harbour Masters House at Kernaghan's Quay, Corry, Belleek. This house and lands were purchased in 1926 by Thomas O'Loughlin, the author's father.

Opposite below: Aerial view of Belleek before the dam was flooded in the early 1950s. Shows the Old Bridge, the Battery Fort, the Pottery, the Sluice Gates and the Great Northern Railway.

A view of Belleek from 'McBrien's Island', about 1935.

Belleek Bridge and the Battery, around 1890. Observe the young man leaning on the parapet enjoying the view and listening to the voice of the River Erne.

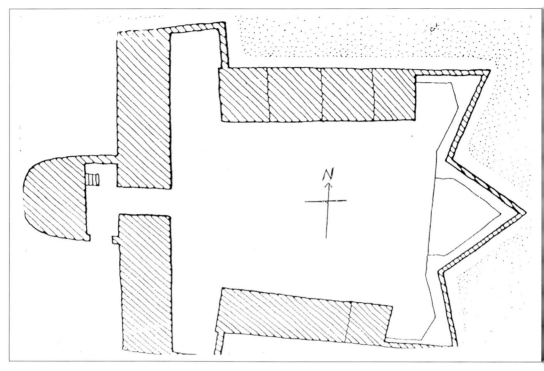

The plans for the Redoubt Fort.

Looking upstream from the bridge towards the Sluice Gates.

A sketch by Horace Fleming of Cora Dermot/Johnston Eel Weir with Cliff House in the Background.

Cora Monagh, Cora Bawn & Cora Donnel the three eel weirs at the Knather, two miles down stream from Belleek, 1946.

View of Belleek village around 1890. Belleek means the 'Place of the Flagstone Ford'. The shallow part of the water would be the ford, it has slopping banks on each side suitable for people or horses crossing.

Camlin Castle, home of the Tredenick family, demolished during the Erne Hydro–Electric Scheme in the 1950s. The Castle was one of three designed by the architect J B Keane. Magheramena Castle, Belleek

and Necarne Castle, Irvinestown were the other two. Only Necarne is still preserved.

Laputa Falls and the Captains Pool, midway between Belleek and Ballyshannon.

Laputa House with its walled garden and the fall. In the field between the garden and the fall, on 2 March 1802, a duel was fought between Lieutenant McGovern and Lawyer Henderson. They were in dispute over an actress. Lt McGovern was killed and he is buried at St Anne's Church, Ballyshannon.

Cora Shane Eel Weir, Ballyshannon Town and its multi arched bridge. On the sky line centre is St Anne's Church.

A view of Ballyshannon from St Anne's Church, the Eel Weir can be seen; less clear is Kathleen's Falls. William Allingham the poet is buried in St Anne's Cemetery.

Kathleen's Falls now replaced by the generating station of the same name.

The Kathleen Fall's ESB Generating Station, not as pleasing to the eye as the Falls.

The famous Assaroe Falls where the river meets the sea. The tidal waters reached the falls and salmon would wait for the high tide before jumping the falls.

Downey's shore at Lowery Bane, about three miles upstream from Belleek. It was from here that the United Irishman, Hugh Ward made his unsuccessful attempt to swim to Roscor Island while trying to escape from Sir John Caldwell's Yeomen. See the top of Breesy Hill and the tower of Oughterdrum Church on skyline.

Deadman's or Lonesome Island where the body of Hugh Ward was buried following his shooting by the Yeomen in 1899.

An upright stone that may have marked the grave of the United Irishman. 'Boots' the dog keeps watch.

Bill Thornhill, whose father, Eddie won in the courts the right for local people to have free trout fishing on the River Erne, around 1890. Bill was an expert fisherman; he had a great pair of hands with which he repaired watches, clocks, gramophones and fishing rods.

Erne Fishery Company.

No *121*

Ballyshannon, *29ᵗʰ May* 189*7*

Thos Beacom Belleek has

permission, from the date hereof *29ᵗʰ May 18.97* to the *19ᵗʰ* day

of *Augt*, 189*7*, to ANGLE for TROUT, and other Fish, save Salmon and Eels, with Hook and Line only, in the River Erne, from the Bar of Ballyshannon to the Distillery Quay, and from the Eel Weir above the Bridge at Ballyshannon upwards, on the Fishery of the Licensors, in the Counties of Donegal and Fermanagh.

Should any of the Conditions on the Back hereof be not complied with, this permission forthwith ceases.

Thos Brun

For the Proprietors of the Erne Fisheries.

A copy of a trout fishing permit issued on behalf of The Erne Fishery Company to Thomas Beacon, Grocer, Main Street, Belleek on 29 May, 1897.

Pat Gallagher and his magic fly. Illustration by Jane O'Loughlin. Obviously Pat did not need a fishing permit and had no fear of the bailiff!

'Ye Killdoney Lads' – the first boat to cast nets on the Erne Estuary, in August 1933. They had won a legal battle against the Erne Fishery Company for the right to fish for salmon under license. From left to right: Willie Morrow, Joe Morrow, Nick Scanlon, 'Red Willie' Goan, Bob Scanlon and Hugh Gavigan. Killdoney is a point on the northwest shore of the estuary, all salmon returning to the Erne to spawn must swim around this point. Shoals of salmon are led by a mature fish known as 'The School Master'. A Belleek fisherman/poacher would never claim to have caught a salmon; rather he would say he caught a 'Killdoney Man'!

A Gillie/boatman and angler trout fishing at the Poll na Hagh pool, under the Battery.

The Horace Fleming Collection

Fishing boats on the Shore at Quinn's House, Magheramena.

An Erne valley sunset with an unusual cloud formation. Taken near the home of the author.

The Barron thatched cottage at Keenaghan Lough.

The Battery and the Sluice Gates from upstream.

The Yew Tree rapids and Fishing Throw. The Daly residence on skyline, birthplace of Dr Edward Daly, Bishop of Derry. The RUC Station and St Patrick's Church also in view.

The rapids below the Great Northern Railway Bridge, with the RUC Police Station in the skyline.

Opposite above: The Yew Tree rapids from the railway bridge with the Battery labourers cottages on the sky line. These were the first public houses built by the county councils of Ireland in the early 1900s.

Opposite below: The Yew Tree Pool.

The White Cat Cove.

The Black Cat Cove.

An Angler ties flies to his cast. Each cast had three flies for trout fishing; only one larger hook was used with a salmon fly. A popular bait for salmon fishing was the blackhead worm.

An Angler sketching the scenery near Heronshaw House. Near him was 'The Captain's Cave'.

Mackey's Heronshaw Guest House. Now the residence of Michael McGrath and family.

A group of fishermen at Heronshaw, around 1950. From left to right: Jack Dickson, Bob Johnston, Arthur Dickson, Mr Moore, Bill Martin, Billy Maxwell and Fred Wilson.

The rapids below the railway bridge.

The rapids below Poll na Hagh Pool and the Coole.

Cora Dermott or Johnston's Eel Weir. This Weir is on the border between Fermanagh and Donegal.

A pair of Erne swans.

Boats at rest on the estuary when the tide was out.

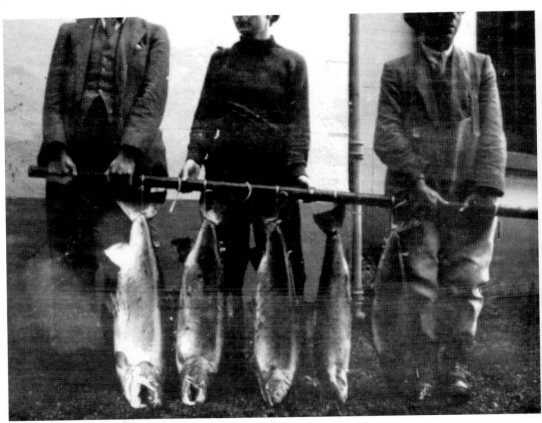

A friend with Eileen and Walter Slater and five fine salmon, a normal catch on the Erne at Belleek.

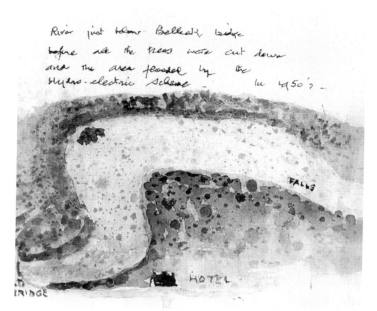

River just below Belleek bridge before all the trees were cut down and the area flooded by the Hydro-electric Scheme — in 1950's —

FALLS

HOTEL

BRIDGE

A Horace Fleming sketch of the Erne below Belleek.

A Fairy Tree near Belleek. Anyone cutting down a fairy tree will do so at their peril. Local people would never interfere with these trees.

One of the three Knather Eel Weirs.

Counting the camera man – a dozen fishermen at the Coole, Belleek. Just down stream from the Carlton Hotel.

Ernie McBrien and Fred Slater display a fine catch of salmon.

The same tree in Four Seasons – Spring.

Summer.

Autumn.

Winter.

The Author at ease. Photo by Anne Cassidy, Enniskillen.

The River Erne above the water falls with the 'Barr of Wealt' in the background. Now on the top of the Barr is the well known Lough Navar view point.

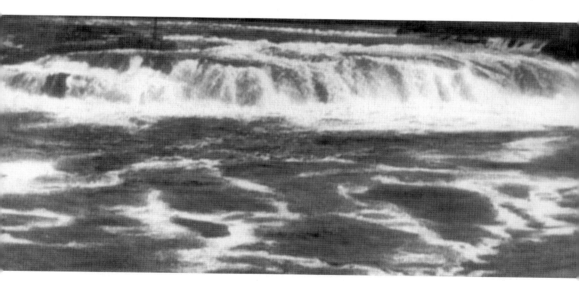

River Erne waterfall, similar to the Belleek Falls.

The Mill Wheel that drove the machinery in Belleek Pottery.

The railway extension into Belleek Pottery.

Main Street, Belleek looking westwards.

Main Street, Belleek looking eastwards.

Market day in Belleek, around 1930.

Magheramena Castle, home of the Johnston family until 1917.

Constable Edward Finn, Royal Irish Constabulary, Belleek, with his wife Bridget, around 1900.

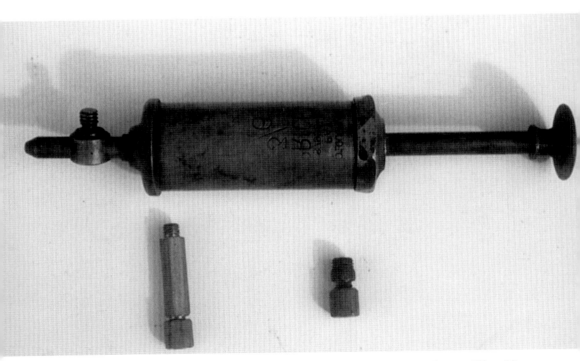

The lubrication pump and firings that were installed on all new bicycles sold by Thomas O'Loughlin.

Grace Little. Ballyshannon.

A stylish hat, around 1900.

Thomas O'Loughlin, Cycle and Motor Agent, Main Street, Belleek. He invented and designed a lubrication system for bicycles.

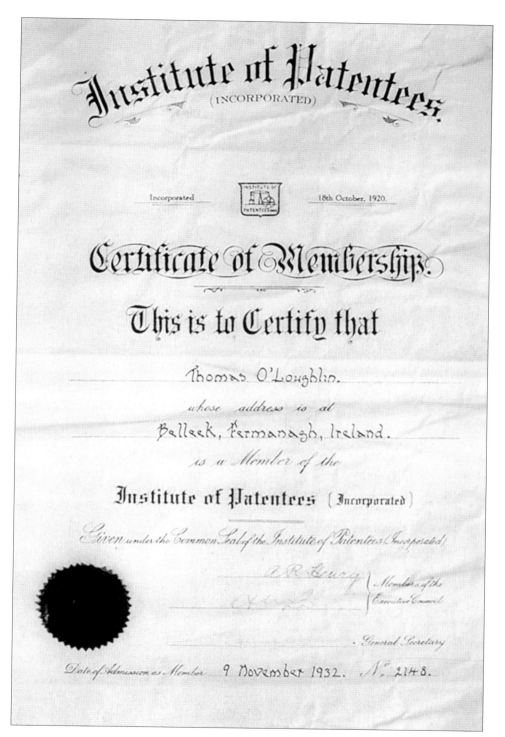

Institute of Patentees.
(INCORPORATED)

Incorporated   18th October, 1920.

Certificate of Membership.

This is to Certify that

Thomas O'Loughlin.

whose address is at

Balleek, Fermanagh, Ireland.

is a Member of the

Institute of Patentees (Incorporated)

Given under the Common Seal of the Institute of Patentees (Incorporated)

A. R. Leary } Members of the Executive Council

. General Secretary

Date of Admission as Member   9 November 1932.   Nº 2148.

Thomas O'Loughlin's Certificate of Membership for the Institute of Patentees.

An Austin Open touring motor car of the early 1930s.

Above: Revd Fr Lorcain O'Ciaran (Parish Priest in Pettigo and Belleek) at his residence, Magheramena Castle.

Right: A visitor to Belleek — former world heavy weight boxing champion Floyd Patterson — with Nora O'Loughlin.

Opposite below: Jock Slevin in his open horse car at Belleek Pottery, early 1900s.

Fr O'Ciaran – third from left with hat and smoking pipe with a group of clerical friends at Maghermena Castle in the early 1930s.

Above left: Another important visitor to Belleek, Her Excellency President Mary McAleese being greeted by the High Sheriff for County Fermanagh – Lord Erne and Mrs McGonnigle, owner of Shannagh Nursing home.

Above right: William John O'Loughlin of the Acres posses for an American visitor on the Main Street, in the mid 1950s.

'Thar She Blows' not an oil well. It is a successful drilling for water on Rathmore Hill, Belleek.

Three Belleek gents enjoy a day out in Bundoran. From left to right: Daniel Murray of Bonahill, Edward Keenan of the Acres and Danny Murray of the Commons.

Workmen, policemen and local business men at the drilling, in the 1930s. From left to right: Erne Elliot, Constable Hasson, Eric Arnold, the contractor, Constable Fox, Bob McBrien, Johnny McCann,

Mick Branley, James Bogle, Tommy O'Loughlin, Frank O'Riley and Billy Stinston, water engineer.

The Revd Nigel Kirkpatrick, a native of Belleek. Now Church of Ireland rector in County Down.

Right: Dr Edward Daly, Bishop of Derry. A native of Belleek now retired. He still lives in Derry.

Opposite: Monsieur Thady Rooney, Long Island, New York a native of Belleek. Monsieur Thady was a prisoner of war in Japanese custody in Thailand during the Second World War.

Joe O'Loughlin and Irvinestown historian, Breege McCusker with a life size replica of the Clogher Cross. This fourteenth century cross was discovered in Slawin, Toura about 1890 and presented to the Clogher Diocese. The original is in the diocesan museum in Monaghan. It is one of the few artifacts in the possession of the Church.

The author with James Nelson. Jimmy was reared in the only thatched building now left in Belleek. He was blind from birth and while on walks with his uncle every part of the landscape was described to Jimmy by Uncle Billy Dolan. With the result that Jimmy could describe the area better than any sighted person. Jimmy's favourite pastime was to walk unaided the few yards from his home to the O'Loughlin bicycle shop where he listened intently to the news of the day being discussed. He knew by sound who owned every cart or motor car that traveled into the village.

The late Eugene Judge a native of Cashel, County Fermanagh with his ever reliable form of transport.

The Penal Days Mass Rock at the Altars, Cashelard, near Breesy Mountain.

James Richard Timoney, Professor of Mathematics, University College Dublin., with his wife Nora and family. Richard, an uncle of the author was a native of Teiranagher, Roscor, Belleek.

Members of the Cashelard Community Association at the unveiling of a memorial stone to mark the site.

The author with two former school comrades, from left to right: Dr Joseph Duffy, Bishop of Clogher and Dr Edward Daly, Bishop of Derry.

A young John Paul Gallagher at the Oughterdrum Mass Rock which is situated half way between Oughterdrum Church of Ireland and St Michaels Church, Mulleek.

Vincent Freeburn at the entrance to the Mass Rock site at the stone he helped to erect to mark this historic place.

Two English visitors Charles and Finula Easthope at the Mass Rock.

Market Day in Belleek in the 1970s.

The McBrien family cottage, Cloghore at the bottom of the Battery Road. Keowns Estate Agency is now on the site.

Grayson's lime kiln at the side of the Commons Road.

An aerial view of Belleek village showing the Pottery, the Bridge and the Erne River, in 1973.

The Lincolnshire – A British Army Regiment prepares to leave Belleek after the establishment of the border in the 1920s.

The army supervise an eviction of premises at Main Street in the 1920s.

The British Army prepares to vacate the Battery Fort in the 1920s.

A ferry pontoon takes a group of officials, an armoured truck and police officers across the river at Roscor before the new bridge was built in 1926.

A group of locals wait to board a train at Belleek Railway Station.

The Lincolnshire's on parade before departing from Belleek.

A Crossly lorry ready to depart from the Battery Fort. See the cook in his white coat!

An army carriage outside a hut in the Battery Fort. This hut would not have been officer's quarters.

Oughterdrum Church of Ireland, now disused. This was the scene of a visit by the Bishop of Clogher after he had received complaints that the Rector, Revd James Benson Tuttle had lost the support of the most of his congregation. The Bishop came to see for himself the dwindling congregation with the intentions of dismissing Tuttle from his post. However his friend Fr Neil Ryan devised a plan to help in the situation. He had his Mass early in St Michaels and brought his flock up to the Church to welcome his Lordship the Bishop, giving the impression that they were all loyal Protestants. The Bishop was so amazed by the devotion of the congregation that the Revd Tuttle was assured of his job for ever more.

Right: An artist's impression of the welcome accorded to his Lordship, by Jane O'Loughlin.

Below: American GI Speedy Jones, who was stationed at Magheramena US radio station, demonstrates how to treat a horse. (also by Jane O'Loughlin)

Over a hundred years ago a local law breaker was sentenced to a month in Sligo or a fine of a pound for some minor misdemeanor. He was dispatched to jail in a jarveys car with a policeman for escort. Having deposited the prisoner in the jail the two men retired to a local pub for some refreshments. The miscreant on entering the jail paid the pound fine to the Warden and was released. He got a lift to Belleek and was standing at Cleary's Corner to greet his escort on their return. (artist Jane O'Loughlin)

Does this faithful hound wait for his master to emerge from a pub?

This is how dogs are treated in Belleek!

Above: The rapids on the River Erne just below Belleek.

Middle: Ballyshannon Mall Quay, where many emigrants departed for the New World.

Right: The Battery Fort in the winter of 1949.

Above: A Giants Grave at Killybegs about three miles from Belleek.

Left: A Standing Stone at the same site.

Right: An unusual and rare stone window frame in the ruins of Keenaghan Church. Efforts to have the authorities preserve this unique building have so far been unsuccessful.

Below: While not connected to Belleek this bronze fountain monument of the Three Fates was erected in St Stephan's Green, Dublin by the German Government in appreciation of the assistance given to their people in their time of need after the Second World War.

The Hotel Carlton, Belleek Pottery, the Bridge and Sluice Gates, around 1890.

A number of guests on the lawn of the Carlton Hotel, some relaxing, others fishing, around 1900.
(Picture courtesy of David Johnson)

T P O'Connell, Bundoran with his beautifully restored Austin Saloon.

The village pump and water trough, Main Street, Belleek.

Left: Trotting to the fair. Going past the home of the late James Nelson.

Below: A sedate Sedan passes by the same house now the 'Thatch Coffee Shop'.

The late James McGonnigle and Patrick Slevin whose collective memories preserved much of the history of the area.

The late Ivan Montgomery and the late Ned Ruddy, two Scotchmen domiciled in Belleek.

The Dispensary House, Main Street. One of the first slated buildings to be erected in the village. Now the residence of the McEniff family.

Opposite above: Men of a past age – Michael Knox, Joe Slevin and Michael McCauley.

Opposite below: The beautifully rebuilt Hotel Carlton, owned by the Johnston family.

Necarne Castle, Irvinestown. The third Keane designed Castle in the Erne valley.

The Duffy farmhouse near Belleek, 1970.

Opposite above: A traditional country farmhouse.

Opposite middle: Golfing in Bundoran in the 1940s.

Opposite below: David Elliott's business premise's around 1900.

Merwyn H Peters, ex-US Navy (Second World War), has a foot on each side of the border on the bridge over the Erne at Belleek.

The young and not so young John McGee at Main St, Belleek.

Right: The late Thomas Duffy, whose farm outside Belleek, had fields in three town lands – Finner, Rathmore and Commons.

Below: Una McGarrigle, Cashelard, County Donegal in the centre with friends on the summit of Breesy Mountain which over looks the Erne Valley. In keeping with a custom going back generations it has been a tradition for people from the district to make the climb to the top of the mountain on the second Sunday of June.

Above left: Hugh Kelly, Corlea, his father a native of County Clare, worked as a stonemason at the building of St Patrick's Church, Belleek in 1891.

Above right: Professor of Mathematics, University College, Dublin. James Richard Timoney. A native of Tieranagher, Roscor, Belleek. (uncle of the author).

Left: Brotherly love. Corlea in the 1940s.

Opposite above: Band leader, Tony Keown with St Mary's Pipe Band – Garrison, on parade at Belleek sports, *c.* 1950.

Opposite below: 'A Tight Squeeze' as Davy Smith makes a delivery of petrol to O'Loughlin's Filling Station!

Above left: Contemplating the next move, Frank Maguire, The Battery.

Above right: Barney McGrory - One man and his dog!

Above left: Barney Collins, 'Dressed to kill' in the style of the 1920s!

Above right: A real Irish lady – Mary Ann McGowan. (by Jane O'Loughlin)

A fair day scene on Belleek Main Street, in the early 1900s.

'I was told to go to *Gate One*'!

Ready for 'Take off to foreign parts'!

A stone quern found
on the O'Loughlin
farm, Acres, Belleek.
Now in the Fermanagh
County Museum, Castle
Barracks, Enniskillen.

Above: Father knows best, as mother relaxes!

Left: The last Great Northern Railway train to leave Belleek for Bundoran in September 1956.

THE FLYING BOATS ON LOUGH ERNE

For a short period in historical terms, Lower Lough Erne developed a new voice; this was during the Second World War, when the *Sunderland* and *Catalina* Flying Boats were based there. This proud lake played a most important part in the 'Battle of the Atlantic'. When the battle was won, the lake once more became silent. Let it tell its own story.

THE FLYING BOATS ON LOUGH ERNE

I still lie here, beneath the hill
Abandoned now, to natures will
My hangers down; gone; my people all
The only sound; the wild birds call

But my mighty 'birds' shall rise no more
I do not hear the engines roar
And never now, does my bosom feel
The lift of that silver keel

From this ageless hill their voices cast
Thunderous echoes of the past
And still in lonely memory
Their great broad wings sweep down to me

Laughter, sorrow, hope and pain
I shall never know these things again
Emotions that I came to know
Of strange young men so long ago

Who knows as evening shadows meet
Are they with us still? That phantom fleet
And do their ghosts still fly unseen
Across my waters so wide and green

And in the future should the forest tall
Change my face beyond recall
I shall still remember them
My metal birds and long dead men

Now trees grown high, obscure the sky
O! Remember me when you pass by
For atop these curling waves
I was your home in other days.

Other titles published by Nonsuch

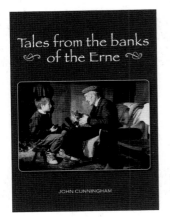

Voices of the Donegal Corridor

JOE O'LOUGHLIN

The Donegal Corridor, based along Lough Erne in County Fermanagh and up the Donegal coast, was a key contribution to the Allies in the Second World War. A place where ally soldiers trained for combat, where planes landed and refuelled and where many crashed and lost their lives. This intriguing book brings together a collection of memories, from home and abroad, of the Donegal Corridor. Joe interviews local people, family members and former comrades. The book is beautifully illustrated with pictures of many of these lost heroes, their aircrafts and the memorial sights of those who never made it home. This book will have a local as well as an international appeal.

1 84588 526 0   £11.49

Tales from the Banks of the Erne

JOHN CUNNINGHAM

A place of great scenic beauty, Loch Erne has long been the inspiration for artists and draws tourists from far and wide. This is a unique collection of tales capturing the experiences and memories of people around the Loch Erne area through the last century, many of which have since passed away. These tales are charming in their humour and simplicity and touching in their honesty. John B. Cunningham is an Irish historian and writer born in County Donegal. He has been gathering and documenting the memories of the older people in the Erne area for some years now and this will form the basis of this enchanting book '*Tales from the Banks of the Erne*'. The collection is illustrated with pictures of the tales many colourful characters.

1 084588 517 1   £11.49

Green Days Cricket in Ireland 1972-2005

GERARD SIGGINS

Irish cricket has a long, colourful history. The earliest photo of an Irish team is an 1858 team group of the Trinity 2nd XI. It was around this time that the game experienced a massive upsurge in interest – cricket was by far the most popular and widely played game in the country until the foundation of the GAA in 1884. By way of illustration, a recent history of cricket in Tipperary shows that at its height in the mid–1880s there were 98 clubs in that county alone. By the 1970s there were none. Designed to appeal to the casual and the hard core follower this book is a must for Irish Cricket fans. Gerard Siggins is the Assistant Editor at The Sunday Tribune and has been a writer and editor of several Cricket magazines over the years.

1 84588 512 0   €17.99

If you are interested in purchasing other books published by Nonsuch, or in case you have difficulty finding any Nonsuch books in your local bookshop, you can also place orders directly through our website

www.nonsuch-publishing.com